I LOVE DAD

I LOVE DAD

Fun Holiday Crafts
Kids Can Do!

Father's Day Crafts

Fay Robinson

Enslow Elementary
an imprint of

Enslow Publishers, Inc.

40 Industrial Road	PO Box 38
Box 398	Aldershot
Berkeley Heights, NJ 07922	Hants GU12 6BP
USA	UK

http://www.enslow.com

Enslow Elementary, an imprint of Enslow Publishers, Inc.

Enslow Elementary® is a registered trademark of Enslow Publishers, Inc.

Library of Congress Cataloging-in-Publication Data

Robinson, Fay.
    Father's Day crafts / Fay Robinson.
        p. cm. — (Fun holiday crafts kids can do)
    Includes bibliographical references and index.
    ISBN 0-7660-2343-5
    1. Holiday decorations—Juvenile literature. 2. Handicraft—Juvenile literature.
3. Father's Day—Juvenile literature. I. Title. II. Series.
TT900.H6R63 2004
745.594'163--dc22

                                            2004010309

Printed in the United States of America

10 9 8 7 6 5 4 3 2

To Our Readers: We have done our best to make sure all Internet Addresses in this book
were active and appropriate when we went to press. However, the author and the publisher
have no control over and assume no liability for the material available on those Internet sites
or on other Web sites they may link to. Any comments or suggestions can be sent by e-mail
to comments@enslow.com or to the address on the back cover.

Illustration Credits: Crafts prepared by June Ponte. © 1996-2004 ArtToday, Inc., p. 4.
                    Photography by Carl Feryok.

Cover Illustration: Carl Feryok

Contents

Safety Note: Be sure to ask for help from an adult, if needed, to complete these crafts!

introduction

It is Father's Day! Dads everywhere get to sleep late. Their families bring them breakfast in bed. They get to be lazy all day if they want. Maybe their families make a special dinner of all their favorite foods.

Mrs. Sonora Smart Dodd was one of the first people to think about a holiday to celebrate fathers. She thought that her father was very special. Her father had to raise his six children by himself after her mother died. Mrs. Dodd thought fathers should have a special holiday just like mothers do on Mother's Day.

Mrs. Dodd's family lived in Washington.

People there thought her idea was a good one. Mrs. Dodd's father was born in June, so the first Father's Day was celebrated in June.

People in other states also thought a special day for fathers was a good idea. In 1966, Father's Day became an official national holiday. Every year it is celebrated on the third Sunday in June.

Coffee Cup Coaster

Lots of dads drink coffee or tea. Does yours? If so, he will love this coaster for holding his cup.

What You Will Need:

- markers
- small plastic lid from a food container
- felt
- scissors
- white glue
- ric-rac, thin ribbon, or yarn

1. Use a marker to trace a circle around the plastic lid on the felt. Cut it out. Put the felt circle inside the lid. Trim it to fit.

2. Glue the felt circle to the inside of the lid.

3. Use the markers to write something or draw a simple picture in the circle.

4. Run a thin line of glue around the outside edge of the lid. Glue on some ric-rac, ribbon, or yarn to decorate the coaster.

Safety Note: Be sure to ask for help from an adult, if needed, to complete these crafts!

Cut the felt to fit
the plastic lid . . .

DAD

Decorate the felt . . .

Use some ric-rac,
ribbon, or yarn for
the finishing touches!

DAD

Holiday Hint:

Now when your dad drinks
coffee or tea, he will have a
special place to put his cup
that will make him think of
you!

King-for-a-Day Crown

Help your dad feel like a king today!

What You Will Need:

- pencil
- construction paper in different colors
- scissors
- tape measure
- white glue
- markers
- glitter, sequins

1. Use the patterns on pages 26 and 27. Trace the crown shapes on construction paper. Cut them out.

2. Next, cut out a band in a different color. It should each be 11 inches long. Glue the band to the crown shape as shown.

3. Glue the pieces of the crown together to make a long strip. Let the glue dry.

4. Use markers, construction paper shapes, glitter, sequins, or whatever you have to decorate the crown.

5. Glue the ends together to make a circle as shown.

Cut the shape for
the crown. . .

Add some different
colored paper . . .

Decorate with
glitter and sequins
to make it special!

Holiday Hint:

At breakfast, tell your dad that you
are crowning him king. As king, he
should wear the crown all day so
people will know he is special!

Cool Comb

Whether your dad's hairstyle is cool or not, this comb will help!

What You Will Need:

- clean plastic comb
- newspaper
- acrylic paint in different colors
- paintbrush

1. Place the comb on newspaper.
2. Paint stripes, hearts, sports equipment, or other designs on the comb for decoration. You could also write your dad's name or his initials on it.
3. Let the paint dry completely.

Use newspaper
to protect
your work
surface...

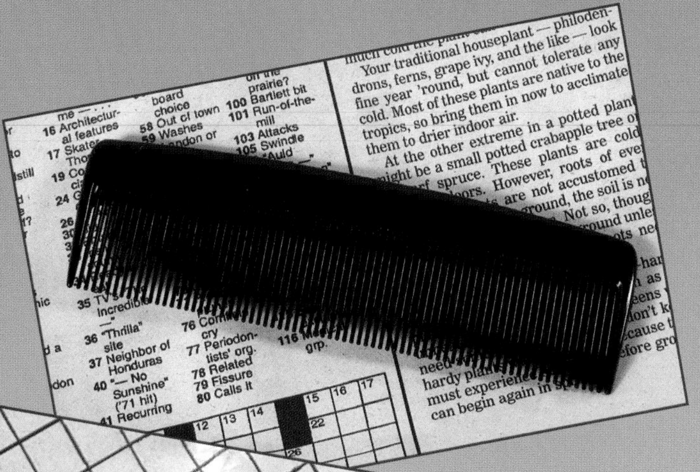

DAD

Use different colored
paint to decorate the
comb!

Holiday Hint:

Make Dad two combs, one
for home and one to take
with him.

I Love Dad Tiepin

Make a tiepin for your dad to wear on Father's Day.

What You Will Need:

- poster board (or heavy paper)
- ruler
- fine-line colored markers
- scissors
- white glue
- paper
- large safety pin

1. On a piece of poster board, about 1½-inches around, write "I Love Dad." Or you can draw a picture instead. This is your tiepin. Make it small so that it will fit on your dad's tie.

2. Cut out your tiepin.

3. Put a thick coat of glue over the tiepin. Make sure the glue goes all the way to the edges. Let the glue dry.

4. Cut a small strip of paper about ¼-inch by ½-inch. Slip the strip of paper between the metal parts of a closed safety pin as shown.

5. Spread glue on the back of the tiepin. Place the strip of paper and the pin into the glue. Make sure the pointy part of the pin is not covered with glue. Let the glue dry overnight.

Safety Note: Be sure to ask for help from an adult, if needed, to complete these crafts!

Write your message on
some poster board . . .

Carefully cut it out . . .

I LOVE DAD

I LOVE DAD

Attach the
safety pin. . .

I LOVE DAD

your pin is ready
to give to your Dad!

Holiday Hint:

On father's Day, help your dad
put on the tiepin. He will be
proud to wear your very
special gift!

A Penholder for Dad

If your dad is like most dads, he leaves pens all over the place. But when he needs one, he can never find one.

What You Will Need:

- empty container that is shorter than a pen
- construction paper in different colors
- scissors
- white glue
- markers

1. Measure a rectangle of construction paper by rolling your container one full circle around on the construction paper. Cut out the rectangle.

2. Glue the paper rectangle on your container. Trim to fit, if necessary.

3. Cut out five or six tie shapes using the patterns on page 29. Choose construction paper that matches the colors of your dad's favorite ties.

4. Use markers to decorate the ties. First draw a line under the knot as shown. Then, draw a different design on each tie. Use stripes, polka dots, plaids, or other patterns.

5. Glue the ties to the container. Place them in a fun design around it.

First, glue construction paper to the outside . . .

Cut out tie shapes in other colors . . .

Glue on the ties and add more decoration!

Holiday Hint:

Go around your home and pick up any of Dad's pens you can find. Put them in the penholder. He will really like having a special place for all of his pens.

Sit-Upon Cushion

Does your dad come to watch you play sports at school? Bleacher seats can feel cold and hard! Help your dad feel more comfortable by making this cushion for him to use.

What You Will Need:

- newspapers
- extra-strength plastic garbage bag
- scissors
- regular clear tape
- packaging clear tape
- acrylic paints (optional)
- paintbrush (optional)

1. Neatly stack newspapers about an inch thick as shown.

2. Press the newspapers into a corner of the garbage bag. Cut around the newspapers on the other sides of the garbage bag as shown. Leave about an inch of the plastic bag.

3. Fold the cut ends of the plastic bag over the newspapers. Use the regular clear tape on the ends to hold them down in place. Make sure the plastic bag is tightly wrapped around the newspapers!

4. Use the clear packaging tape to make a framelike seal around all four sides. Cut down the edges of the plastic bag if they hang over the tape.

Gather up a stack of newspapers . . .

Cover the stack with a garbage bag . . .

Add some artwork and your cushion is ready!

Holiday Hint:

To make this sit-upon special, decorate the cushion with acrylic paint.

Desk Pal

Does your dad work at a desk? He might like to have a desk pal to keep him company.

What You Will Need:

- • pipe cleaners
- • ruler
- • wiggle eyes or a picture of you to cut up (Get permission first!)
- • white glue

1. To make the body and legs of the desk pal, fold one pipe cleaner in half. Fold the bottom ends up to make feet.

2. Take a second pipe cleaner and fold it in half. Leaving about an inch at the top for the head, wrap the two ends around the body.

3. When you have about 2 inches left on each end, make arms. Fold them to make elbows and hands as shown.

4. To make the head, open the top loop to make a round shape. Take another pipe cleaner and wrap it around.

5. You can add pants and a shirt by wrapping other pipe cleaners around the legs, body, and arms. Wrap a short piece of pipe cleaner around the top of the head for hair.

6. Cut out a picture of yourself and glue it on the head. If you do not have a picture, use wiggle eyes to make a funny face.

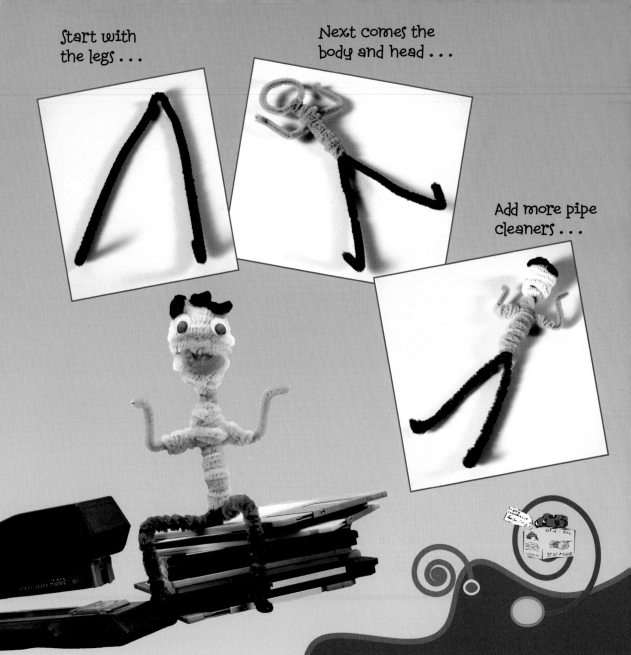

Start with the legs . . .

Next comes the body and head . . .

Add more pipe cleaners . . .

Your desk pal is ready for display!

Holiday Hint:

Fold the desk pal at the knees and hips as shown. Then adjust it so it sits on the edge of your dad's desk.

19

iOU Book

How can you help your dad? Make an IOU (I owe you—get it?) book. Tell him all the things you will help him do during the year.

What You Will Need:

- masking tape
- scissors
- 2 index cards
- brown watercolor paint
- paintbrush
- construction paper in different colors
- markers
- hole punch
- yarn or ribbon

1. Cut several small pieces of masking tape. Stick them on one side of each index card. Stick the tape pieces down any way you want.

2. Trim any ends of tape hanging over the cards.

3. Paint the tape with brown watercolor that is not too watery. This will make an interesting leathery look for the covers. Let the paint dry.

4. Cut pieces of construction paper the same size as the index cards. These will be your IOUs.

5. Think of things you can do for your dad. Write each one on an IOU with the markers. For example, "IOU an afternoon of help washing the car," or "IOU one week of emptying the garbage."

6. Punch two holes in one of the covers. Trace the holes on each IOU and the other cover so that the holes line up. Punch the holes in one piece at a time.

7. Put yarn or ribbon through the holes and tie in a bow.

Make the front and back covers . . .

Write IOUS . . .

IOU
ONE AFTERNOON
OF HELP WASHING
THE CAR

IOU
ONE DAY OF YARD
WORK

DAD

Use yarn to tie it all together!

Holiday Hint:

Make a lot of IOUS. Tell Dad that he can use an IOU whenever he needs help. He will really love this Father's Day gift!

Eyeglass Holder

Does your dad wear eyeglasses? If so, this soft case will keep them from getting scratched.

What You Will Need:

- felt
- marker
- scissors
- white glue
- ric-rac or yarn

1. Use the pattern on page 28. Draw the shape on the felt with a marker. Cut it out.

2. Put a line of glue around three sides of the felt as shown. Do not put glue at the top!

3. Fold the felt in half. Hold it in place for a couple of minutes until the glue dries a little.

4. Glue on ric-rac or yarn to decorate the eyeglass case.

Safety Note: Be sure to ask for help from an adult, if needed, to complete these crafts!

Create the pattern . . .

Carefully cut out the felt and glue two of the edges . . .

DAD

Add decorations and your eyeglass case is ready!

Holiday Hint:

Write "Dad" or his name on the case. Then everyone will know whose eyeglass case it is. Dad and his eyeglasses will both love it!

You Are Framed!

Here is an easy way to make a picture frame for a photograph.

What You Will Need:

- empty CD case
- photograph of you (Get permission first!)
- ruler
- pencil
- scissors
- construction paper
- white glue
- markers or crayons

1. Take the paper out of the CD case.

2. Measure a 3-inch square on the photo. Cut out the photo square.

3. Measure a 4¾-inch square on the construction paper. Cut out the paper square.

4. Glue the photograph in the center of the paper square. Write "I love Dad" all over the paper border.

5. Put the photo in the front part of the CD case. Slide it under the plastic flaps to hold it in place. Put a thin line of glue at the top of the paper. Press the paper to the plastic.

Carefully cut a piece of
construction paper . . .

Empty the
CD case . . .

Place a photograph
in the middle and
decorate!

Holiday Hint:

Show your dad how to
open the frame so it will
stand up. It will look great
wherever he puts it.

Patterns

Use tracing paper to copy the patterns on these pages. Ask an adult to help you cut and trace the shapes onto construction paper.

at 100%

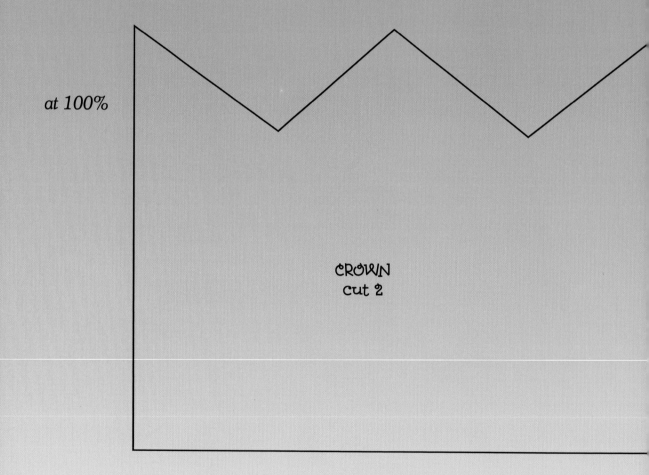

CROWN
cut 2

overlap this end and
tape together to form
center seam

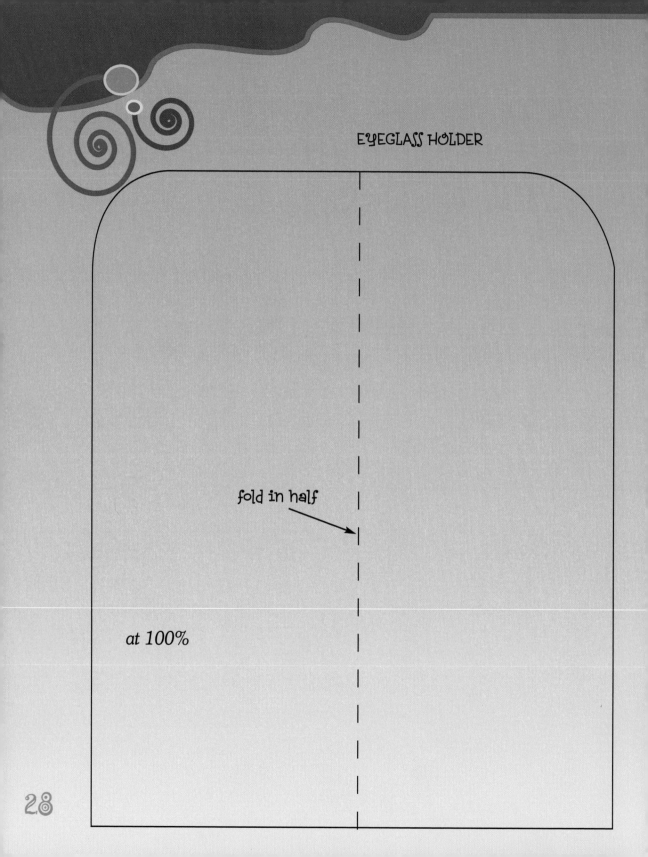

EYEGLASS HOLDER

fold in half

at 100%

Cut as many as you need

at 100%

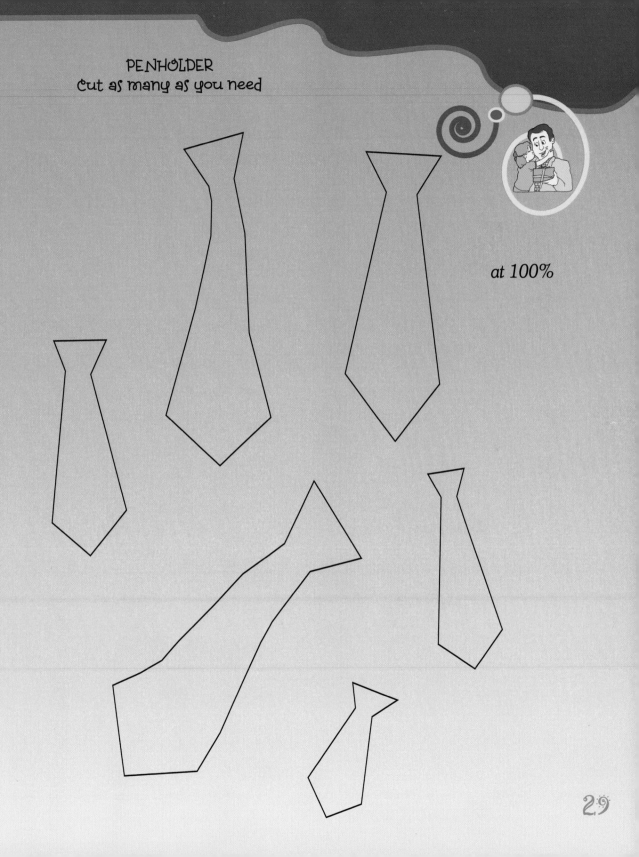

Reading About Father's Day

Auld, Mary. *My Dad*. Milwaukee, Wisc.: Gareth Stevens Pub., 2004.

Nielsen, Shelly. *Celebrating Father's Day*. Minneapolis, Minn.: ABDO Publishing Company, 1996.

Ross, Kathy. *Crafts for All Seasons*. Brookfield, Conn.: Millbrook Press, 2000.

Steptoe, Javaka. *In Daddy's Arms I am Tall: African Americans Celebrating Fathers*. New York: Lee & Low Books, 1997.

Zalben, Jane Breskin. *To Every Season: A Family Holiday Cookbook*. New York, Simon & Schuster Books for Young Readers, 1999.

Internet Addresses

BillyBear4Kids: Happy Father's Day

Learn more about Father's Day.

<http://www.billybear4kids.com/holidays/father/dad.htm>

Holidays at Kids Domain

Want to do more for Dad on Father's Day? Check out this site.

<http://www.kidsdomain.com/holiday/dad/>

Index